W9-AFS-650

FIND YOUR TALENT

MAKE AN ANIMATION!

Sarah Levete

ARCTURUS

Children's & Parents' Services
PATCHOGUE-MEDFORD LIBRARY

FIND YOUR TALENT!

Have you ever watched an animated film or TV show and wondered how it was made? Have you ever thought about giving it a try? Well, now is the time to make a start. You will have fun and you may even discover you have a real talent.

Some of the best animation ideas start off as simple sketches.

Trick of the eye!

So what is animation? Animate means "bring to life"—the subject could be a picture, puppet, or toy. In an animation, what you see is a series of still pictures. Each image is slightly different from the one before. It is the speed at which the pictures are shown that tricks the eyes into thinking that the pictures are moving.

Animation is all about tricking the eye into thinking that a still image is moving.

Myth busting

Before you start, we need to get rid of a few myths about animation:

- **You have to be a brilliant artist.** Wrong! You can animate simple stick figures or modeling clay faces. Of course, many animators are fantastic artists but it is not essential.

- **You need the most up-to-date camera and computer.** Wrong! A basic digital camera or scanner and a computer with some simple software will do.

EARLY DAYS: Starting out

Most animators discover their talent for animation at home. For example, two of today's most successful animators began their careers at the kitchen table. Peter Lord and Dave Sproxton's first animation was a chalk figure on a blackboard. For each frame, the young hopefuls rubbed out a bit of the chalk, redrew it and shot it again. They then repeated the process again and again! Today, Peter Lord and his childhood friend run the hugely successful Aardman Animations, makers of films such as the hilarious *Chicken Run*.

Animating models made out of clay is called claymation.

Let's go! From drawings to action toys, you can bring anything to life. Well, not quite literally to life, but you get the picture! Over the next few pages, you will see just how easy animation can be.

MOVING PICTURES

Many animators start off by making flipbooks or flickbooks. These are "books" made from a series of pictures or photographs that each change slightly. When you flip the pages, the pictures appear to move.

INSIDE STORY: SIMON'S CAT

Inspired by his favorite cartoons, British animator Simon Tofield began making flipbooks when he was very young. He uploaded his first animations onto the video-sharing web site YouTube. The word spread and Simon's animations about his four cats received thousands of hits. Since then, *Simon's Cat* has been turned into books and a cartoon in a national newspaper.

Any sequence of movements, such as these old film images, can be joined together in a flipbook to create a moving picture.

Flipped out pictures The best way to start animating is by making your own flipbook out of a simple sequence or action. This sequence could be anything, such as a figure kicking a ball or a ball bouncing down some stairs. This will give you a sense of how pictures appear to move and how each frame in an animation needs to work.

Why not make your own flipbook? All you need are about 24 small sheets of paper (all the same size), a bulldog clip and a pencil or pen:

- Use the bulldog clip to fasten the sheets of paper together on one side. These will be your frames.
- Draw the first image in your sequence on the first sheet of paper. Keep the image toward the open edge of the pad so you will be able to see it when you flick the pages.
- Change the image slightly in each drawing—you will need about 24 frames for the effect of movement.
- Hold the bulldog clip, flip with your thumb, and watch the action in motion. This is the start of your animation adventure!
- When you feel confident, you could try putting photographs of a model that you have moved in each frame onto the pages.

By studying the movements of people in real life, animators can recreate them in their characters.

Animate all the key stages in the movement of a subject, then watch it come to life!

THE BASICS

You've seen how easy it is to create a moving picture with a flipbook. Now, it's time to get to grips with the basic process of animation.

Many animators start off by drawing their characters before moving onto other media.

GO FOR IT: STEP-BY-STEP

These are the key stages in making an animation:

- Brainstorm to find an idea for your animation.
- Choose your medium.
- Write a synopsis for your story.
- Make a storyboard. This is a cartoon strip that shows the key parts of the story.
- Start drawing, model-making, or cutting out your images.
- Create a background or set for your characters.
- Photograph every different move you wish your character to make.
- Scan the images or upload them from a digital camera.
- Add any sound effects or speech.
- Finally, edit the animation.
- Watch, and be amazed!

Touchy feely One of your biggest questions will be whether to draw or use models. Doodle to see whether drawing is for you. Try experimenting with materials such as clay to see if you prefer animating models. Play around with bringing an action toy to life or cut out some paper puppets. For your animation, use whichever medium you enjoy the most.

Where to work Although you do not need a studio, you do need a clear space. A kitchen table is ideal but not if you need to clear your pictures, models, and camera away three times a day for meals! Try to set up where your camera, models, or pictures will not be disturbed or easily knocked. Can you close the curtains or blinds? A dull day or bright sunshine may ruin continuity in your animation.

Early animators created the phenakistoscope. This was a circular device containing images. When spun, the images on the phenakistoscope blended into one moving picture—an animation.

The first photographic animators joined frames of simple movements together to create their animations.

EARLY DAYS: Moving on

In 1872, Eadweard Muybridge experimented with a series of photographs, creating one of the first photographic animations. In the 1930s, drawn animation took off and Walt Disney produced his first full-length animated film, *Snow White and the Seven Dwarfs* in 1937. Computers transformed animation, and Pixar's *Toy Story* became the first feature-length 3D computer-generated animated film. Computer programs have made it much easier for anyone to try their hand at animation.

CLASSICAL STYLE

Let's look at some different types of animation that you could try. Once you've decided which one works for you, you can start to plan your cartoon. First, let's look at classical drawn animation.

Some of the simplest drawn animations are the most effective. You can choose to work either in black and white or in color.

GO FOR IT: START YOUR ART

To start a hand-drawn animation, you will need this equipment:
- A hole punch makes holes at the edge of each piece of paper.
- A peg bar keeps the paper in position for each new drawing. It is a bar with two pegs fixed to it. The pegs go through the punched holes in the paper. If you cannot find a peg bar in your local art shop, you can make your own one. Ask an adult to help you fix two pegs to a wooden ruler.
- A light box lets you see several drawings at once, so that you can easily trace them. You can make your own light box by shining a light under a piece of plexiglas.

Keep it simple Every line in drawn animation needs to be redrawn for each frame, so make life easy! Instead of lots of hair, stick to a few curls. Avoid detail such as logos or numbers on clothes—you will come to hate them if you need to draw them over 12 times for just one second of action! Don't forget to number your pictures.

Time cheat Once you have a feel for drawn animation and want to save time, use cels (transparent sheets of film). First, draw the background onto some paper. Next, draw anything that changes position on the cels. Then, place the cels onto the background.

INSIDE STORY: PENCIL POWER

The very successful animated films *Princess Mononoke* and *Spirited Away* made by Japanese animator Hayao Miyazaki were first drawn by hand in pencil. Miyazaki heads a team of 140 animators at his studios and says, "Those who don't use pencils shouldn't belong to our studio. So they all do!"

This animator is using a light box while studying his face for character inspiration.

JUNKYARD

If you don't want to draw, try animating objects found around your house. You can use anything from toys, such as old action figures, dolls, or building blocks, to fruit, vegetables, and even junk.

Think outside the box Look around your house for old cardboard boxes. By joining together boxes of different sizes you can create a fun character.

Raid the toy box Your old toys are just waiting to be brought to life again! Take a look at cars, balls, toy trains, and other discarded toys. Make sure that the toys can stand up on their own or will stay put with sticky tack.

Animate a figure made from cardboard boxes. Check the limbs stay in position when you move them.

GO FOR IT: TALKING FRUIT AND VEG

It's time to make your fruit talk!:
- Find some fruit or vegetables, such as apples, potatoes, or bananas.
- Use a pen to draw in different expressions on the fruit and vegetables.
- Push pipe cleaners or bendy straws into the fruit and vegetables to make arms and legs.

A Lego car and characters can be used to create a fantastic animation.

Talking toys If you choose toys or models that have movable parts, check that you can move them easily. You can find some amazing examples of animated Lego toys on YouTube. These animations even have their own name—brickfilms.

It's easy to add character and expression to a simple apple.

INSIDE STORY: LEGEND ON FILM

In 2003, a full-length animation called *The Legend of the Sky Kingdom* made it into the top five at the International Animated Film Festival in France. The Zimbabwean filmmakers made their models out of junk, such as scrapped car parts, because that was all they could afford. "The idea of making a movie out of nothing really appealed to me, and I think it fired our creativity and passion in a way that proved you don't need big money and experience—what matters is passion and determination," said director Roger Hawkin.

MAKE YOUR OWN

You can be super creative and make your own models to animate. You do not need elaborate puppets or expensive clays. Instead, use any material—as long as it is flexible and can be moved several times without breaking.

Knitted up Young animator Charlotte Blacker's prize-winning animation called *The Little Red Plane* featured models made from wool. What are you waiting for? Start knitting!

Look for modeling materials in toy or craft shops, which you can use to create your characters.

Woolen characters should be made with a wire "skeleton" inside to support their shape and to make the character's arms and legs movable for animation shots.

Get bendy Modeling clay is great for molding, but it weakens when it gets hot. Take care not to shine bright lights onto it! Bend, twist, push, press, and squash the clay to shape it. Experiment with the feel and shape. For extra support, you could make a frame or skeleton before adding the molding material—bendy wire, foil, or pipe cleaners can all be twisted into a basic shape.

GO FOR IT: READY TO ROLL

Follow these basic tips to make sure your model is shoot-fit:

- Keep the design bold and simple. A fussy design is harder to move or reproduce if it breaks.
- Make sure the model can stand up on its own.
- Check you can move the body parts easily and the arms do not break off every time you change the pose.
- Take care that you don't leave dirty fingerprints on soft materials such as modeling clay.

If you don't like working with clay, you can create fabulous animation characters from plasticine instead.

INSIDE STORY: ALL CHANGE

Clay characters can be manipulated to change shape—and so character—dramatically. The Italian animators at Misseri Studio are famous for changing, or morphing, their clay cat characters from the children's TV animation show Mio Mao. The cats can turn into balls, leaves, and even other animals! Take a look at them in action by typing "Mio Mao" into www.youtube.com.

CUT IT OUT

Cutout animation uses flat puppets made from paper, photos, or materials such as fuzzy felt. This kind of animation does not create smooth movements but it has a charming style.

Can you cut it? A simple shape can be cut out from colored or patterned paper, or you can draw a more detailed character onto a sheet of blank paper, then cut it out.

Move it! Unlike classically sketched characters, cutouts only need to be drawn once. This means you can make your character more detailed than a traditional drawn animation. Once you have created your character, cut it into moveable parts: legs, feet, head, and body.

You can make your cut-out characters from cardboard.

GO FOR IT: THE BEST BITS

Get the best from your cutout:
- Join it by sewing the parts together with a needle and thread. You can also use tape to join the parts together.
- Use tweezers to move only the part of the cutout that you want to move, without moving the whole character.
- To give a character a range of expressions, have several head cutouts with different expressions or have separate eyebrows, eyeballs, and mouths that you can add to your cutout.
- Cover your cutout with sticky-backed plastic to make it last longer. Check that the pieces still move.

In the background For a dramatic, stark look, choose a dark piece of paper for your background. If you go for a funky, patterned background, make sure it does not dominate your cutouts. If you add in props such as toys or models, check they are in proportion to your cutouts.

MIX AND MATCH

INSIDE STORY: Cutouts often suit the style of children's books. The TV cartoon *Charlie and Lola* (based on Lauren Child's books about a brother and sister) blends cutouts, drawings, and fabrics—the books are a mixture of painting, drawing, and collage.

Old fabric can make a fantastic cutout material.

Don't throw away wrapping paper—keep it to create cutouts!

STORY TIME

ow that you have chosen your medium, it is time to put your ideas onto paper. A storyboard will help you work out how your great idea is going to work as an animation.

Is your animation going to be a funny take on a tale or will you give it a more serious treatment?

Find your story If you want to develop a story, it is usually easier to start with something that you know well. You could also choose a scene from a classic fairy tale but give it your own spin. Sometimes, the most unlikely subject matter works—look at the huge success of Bart Simpson's bickering family! Look for inspiration wherever you are. Keep a notebook and pen with you so you can jot down any ideas.

GO FOR IT: WHAT'S THE STORY?

Follow these simple steps to draw a complete storyboard:

- Draw some black frames on paper with space underneath where you can write a summary of the action or any details you want to include once you have your story.
- Break down your tale into a series of images that represent the actions taking place in the story.
- Draw these images roughly onto your storyboard frames.
- Write a simple paragraph that explains what is happening in the boxes below each frame.
- Add in any dialogue or details of other effects (such as sound) that could add to your story and its interest for the viewer.
- Note down how you will film each frame—do you want close-ups, long shots, or do you need to see your character from the side?

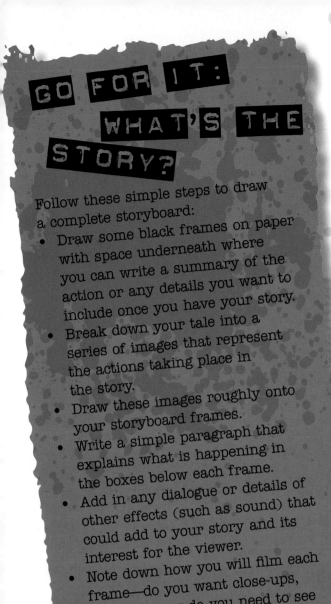

Working through a storyboard with a friend can throw up some great new ideas.

Magic moments A storyboard is like a cartoon strip of the main moments in your animation. Working on it will help you to think about who is telling the story and what you want to show. It is a rough sketch so you do not have to spend time working up each drawing fully. Even if your animation is simple, storyboard it—otherwise you will not know which stages you need to shoot.

EARLY DAYS: Two years of storytelling

Nick Park first developed the concept of the feature-length film *Wallace and Gromit: The Curse of the Were-Rabbit* by writing and drawing ideas with colleague Steve Box. It then took a lengthy two years to storyboard the idea—but it was well worth it!

SHOOT AND LOAD

To get a feel for the process of animation, film a very simple sequence of movements, such as a hand making a fist then opening out again. Look at the camera's manual to find out how you can film a single frame at a time. Use a camcorder, digital camera, or smart phone.

GO FOR IT: STEADY

A camera that wobbles will not work for animation. To avoid wobble:
- Place the camera in front of the model and make sure it is steady.
- Set up a stand or tripod if you have one to keep the camera in place. If you do not have a tripod, set the camera on a pile of books and use some tape to keep it in place.
- For drawings or cutouts (see pages 10–11 and 16–17), fix the camera above the images.

A tripod holds the camera steady.

Stop and move a model again and again to make it look as if it is moving. This is known as stop-motion animation.

Freebies You can use software that comes free with your computer, such as iMovie and Windows Movie Maker, to import your photos and run them as a film. To learn to use the programs, watch a tutorial online. You will be able to edit your animation, deleting frames or adding in extra ones by copying and pasting.

A UNICORN CALLED CHARLIE

INSIDE STORY:

A surreal animation featuring a unicorn called Charlie has had nearly millions of YouTube hits. Jason Steele, creator and animator of this short film says, "I just grab a camera and shoot stuff, or grab a computer and animate. The best way to learn how to make movies is to simply go out and make them."

Some camcorders have a facility that allows you to shoot frames for your animation.

Keep it snappy! Most professional animation is shot at 12 or 24 frames per second (fps). Start off with 12fps—so for every second of film, you need 12 frames or shots. It does not take a math genius to realize that it is a good idea to start with a short animation!

PICTURE PERFECT

Once you have mastered the basics, you can think about fine-tuning your characters and shooting techniques.

Check it out It is important to be consistent with a character. Use a model sheet to keep track of what the character looks like from every angle. Try to draw front, side, and back views of the character, keeping each key part in line so that every view of it is in proportion. Make notes—it is easy to forget the details. Once you have decided on the size of your character, stick to it, unless of course the story involves the character morphing!

Create a record of your character from every angle to ensure the finished detail is perfect.

INSIDE STORY:

BEST-LOVED MOUSE

Mickey Mouse has a unique look that never changes. He always wears red shorts with two buttons on the front, large yellow shoes, and trademark white gloves. This consistency of characterization makes Mickey one of the most recognizable animated characters of all time.

Look at your work to see if you need to add or rework any parts.

GO FOR IT: ALL IN THE ANGLE

To get the most out of filming, experiment with these angles and shot types:

- close-up—use this to emphasize a particular thing in a scene
- cut—a quick change where the shot is suddenly moved to another view
- cross-cut—cut from one action to another to make them look as if they are happening at the same time
- fade—let the image slowly fade from the screen
- long shot—show everything in the scene to give an overview of the character in the setting
- mid-shot—use to focus on the character's actions and words
- pan—let the camera move to a different part of a scene

Angle for effect You can use the camera angle to add atmosphere and mood, and to enhance characterization. If a character walks into a wall in your animation, let the camera wobble! If you want to draw attention to a particular point in your film, use a close-up angle and hold the shot for a second or two for impact.

Different points of view can make your animation more dynamic. A close-up shot can focus on facial expression. A full-body shot can show your character in action.

COMPUTER MAGIC

You can use a computer to both create the frames for your animation and then edit it. If you want to try computer animation, search the Internet for free programs and follow their tutorials.

3D computer animation Some of the major animation successes have been created by computers in three dimensions, or 3D. The animator designs the character but the computer creates the models. Characters are manipulated with the use of complex computer tools. If you want to explore 3D computer animation, you will need a powerful computer and a 3D animation package.

Before you download a program, check it is compatible with your computer system.

Try character creation on your computer—you can get some great results.

GO FOR IT: FIND FREEBIES

Search the Internet for free programs that you can use for 2D computer animation.

- Pencil—for stop-motion or hand-drawn animation (for Mac OS X, Windows, or Linux).
- CreaToon—2D animation software in cutout style (for Windows 95, 98, NT4, ME, 2000, or XP).
- Synfig—animation software (for Windows, Linux, and Mac OS X).
- Blender—2D animation (for Windows, Linux, and Mac OS X).

INSIDE STORY: NOT SO FAST

Many people think that 3D computer animation is super quick to create. Not always! It takes Pixar, the creators of Cars and Monsters, Inc, an average of six hours to render all the different parts that make up just one frame of an animated film. That is the equivalent of more than an astonishing 88 years of rendering for a 90-minute film.

Filling in Key frames are the major start and end points of a move or action, such as a run or a jump. In computer animation, you can use the computer program to add in extra frames between the key frames. This is known as tweening. Once you have created the key frames, you can instruct the computer program to work out the "tweening" frames to go in between.

SOUND IT OUT

Some brilliant animations have no sound at all. Others are transformed by the addition of sound effects or music—and the soundtrack helps the audience to connect with the animation. Search the Internet for free audio downloads or record your own.

Voiceovers If you are giving your characters a voice, it is best to record it before you film. However, you then need to shoot your animation to fit the voice. If you want your character to look as if it is talking, draw the different shapes a person's mouth makes when saying different sounds so that you have some ready reference.

INSIDE STORY: WHO'S SPEAKING?

Who can forget Eddie Murphy's voice for the donkey in Shrek or Angelina Jolie voicing the Tigress in Kung Fu Panda? But when a team first sell their idea for a film, they record the dialogue. Sometimes, they are so good that they actually become the voice of the character for the final film!

Call on your friends to voice your characters and don't be shy about giving some direction!

All you need is a microphone, imagination, and to follow these steps to get the soundtrack right:

- If your computer doesn't have a built-in microphone, you will need to buy or borrow one.
- Search the Internet for free recording and editing programs such as Audacity.
- Think outside the box—if you want to hear the sound of crackling flames, do not start a fire! Instead, scrunch up a potato chip bag. Spin bike wheels for wind and hit a table with a rolled up newspaper for a resounding "thwack!"

Sound effects Add music and other sound effects when you have completed your animation. Until you can see your work, you will not know what the sound "looks like." For example, the sound of something breaking may need a heavy thud or a splintering, tinkling noise.

You can record simple sounds, such as a doorbell, to use in your animation film.

Scrunch up some paper—can you hear that it sounds like feet walking on gravel?

Copyright If you decide to use prerecorded music you need to make sure you are legally allowed to do so. Recorded music is copyrighted. Contact the person or company that owns the license and ask for permission to use it. You may have to pay a fee but it is important to make sure you stay within the law.

STEP UP A GEAR

Master the art of animation and you may be able to carve out a career for yourself!

Now that you have experimented with different animation media and you have made a couple of films, it is time to take your animation to the next level!

Show time! One of the easiest ways to reach a wide audience is through video-sharing web sites such as YouTube, Metacafe, and Dailymotion. You can decide if you want your animation available to anyone and everyone, or if you want to limit it to a select few of your friends. Read the small print though to see who will own the copyright once it is uploaded.

Screen it Arrange a screening for your friends and family. Ask for feedback. Do not take criticism personally! Rather, use their comments to help you to understand what other people like about your animation, and how you can improve it.

Courses There are plenty of classes or workshops you can take to develop your animation skills. Life drawing will help you to draw and create convincing figures with flowing movements. Writing classes will help you to structure and plan your story, and write the script.

Moving along Find out if there is a local animation group or training center near you. Take some courses and then offer to help out. There are often competitions and festivals to enter. An Internet search should help you access the relevant ones.

Make a portfolio If you are really serious about working in animation, you need a show reel or portfolio of your work. Include only the pieces that show your best work, not everything you have ever done. Before you send it to a company, do your research. Lots of companies do not accept unsolicited portfolios. If the company accepts show reels, try to find the name of the person to address it to so you can follow it up with them afterward.

The future Animation is not just about the art of drawing or making a model move. There are so many elements to it. Think about which aspect you enjoy most and which you are best at. Animation companies can have huge teams working on one project, and any one of these roles might suit you:
- director
- storyboard artist
- camera operator
- moving model animator
- key drawing animator (showing the key moves)
- model maker
- studio animator
- computer game animator

GLOSSARY

brainstorm to think of lots of ideas

brickfilms the name given to animations using brick toys such as Lego

cels short for celluloid: the transparent sheets on which animation drawings are traced and painted

claymation characters made from clay, such as Wallace and Gromit

collage using pieces of material or paper to make a picture

compatible works with

continuity consistency of appearance, even when something is filmed on different days

copyrighted when a piece of work is owned by an artist or musician. The owner has the right to refuse or give permission for others to use the work

customize to give an individual look to something

cutouts flat animation figures cut from paper or other material with moveable parts, such as arms or legs

dialogue talking

director the person who has overall control of a project and decides what happens in the filming

edit to cut and move around to improve the overall animation

elaborate complicated

emphasize to draw attention to

fabric material

flexible to be able to move easily

frame a single image in a series of images that move quickly to create the illusion of movement

key frame the start and end point of a move

license permission to use something

manipulated made to move

medium the material you use for animating

model sheet a sheet on which animators record details about each character, from size to look

peg bar a device that holds sheets of paper in position

perspex a see-through, tough plastic

portfolio a collection of your work

proportion to scale

props objects, such as furniture, used in a film or animation

render to turn computer data into visual images

resounding strong, noisy

sequence actions that take place in order

set the props and background used in an animation

show reel your best work presented on film or video

soundtrack a recording to go with a film

stop-motion animation using models

storyboard a cartoon strip that plots the key parts of an animation

surreal fantastical or dreamlike

synopsis a summary of a story

three dimensional, or 3D an image that has height, width, and gives the impression of depth

tripod a three-legged stand used to hold a camera steady

tweening when computer software creates the frames inbetween key frames

two dimensional, or 2D an image that has height and width

unsolicited not asked for

upload to transfer data onto a computer

FURTHER INFORMATION

Books

The Animation Book: A Complete Guide to Animated Filmmaking—From Flip-Books to Sound Cartoons to 3-D Animation by Kit Laybourne (Three Rivers Press, 1998)

Beginner's Guide to Animation: Everything You Need to Get Started by Mary Murphy (Watson-Guptill, 2008)

Cartoons and Animations by Richard Spilsbury (Heinemann/Raintree, 2007)

The Klutz Book of Animation: How to Make Your Own Stop-Motion Movies by Nicholas Berger (Klutz, 2010)

Web sites

You can find some fascinating web sites to help you become familiar with animation generally, or with a particular type of animation.

Cartoonster
This great site provides free online lessons in how to animate, giving you short cuts and insiders' secrets along the way.
www.cartoonster.com

Karmatoons
Here's a chance to learn how to do classic animation, like those early Walt Disney movies.
www.karmatoons.com

INDEX

DISCARD
EXC

JUL 1 0 2014